978341

152.4
Cro

Croft, Priscilla
Dealing with jealousy

10.46

MW00909555

DATE DUE	BORROWER'S NAME	

978341

152.4
Cro

Croft, Priscilla
Dealing with jealousy

MEDIALOG INC
ALEXANDRIA KY 41001

The Conflict Resolution Library

Dealing with Jealousy

• Priscilla Croft •

The Rosen Publishing Group's
PowerKids Press
New York

Published in 1996 by The Rosen Publishing Group, Inc.
29 East 21st Street, New York, NY 10010

First Edition

Book design: Erin McKenna

Photo Credits: Cover © Dusty Willison/International Stock; p. 12 courtesy of the McKenna family; p. 16 © Mimi Cotter/International Stock; p. 19 © Barry Elz/International Stock; all other photos by Matt Harnet.

Croft, Priscilla
    Dealing with jealousy / Priscilla Croft. — 1st ed.
        p.   cm. — (The conflict resolution library)
    Includes index.
    Summary: Discusses the emotion jealousy and suggests ways of handling this difficult feeling.
    ISBN 0-8239-2326-6
    1. Jealousy—Juvenile literature. [1. Jealousy.] I. Title. II. Series.
    BJ1535.J4J64   1996
    152.4—dc20   95-48383
                                                                              CIP
                                                                               AC

Manufactured in the United States of America

Contents

What Is Jealousy?

Jealousy (JEL-us-see) is an **emotion** (ee-MOH-shun), like happiness or sadness or anger. When you are jealous, you want something that someone else has.

You might feel jealous when something good happens to someone you know, like your best friend or your brother or sister. You may wish that the good thing had happened to you. Instead of feeling happy for that person, you may be angry or upset with him or her.

◄ A person may feel jealous when something good happens to someone else.

Winner's Luck

Talia had helped her mom bake cookies. She couldn't wait to share them with her best friend, Shawna, that day. But Shawna had some exciting news of her own. "I won a free pass to the skating rink!" she said. Ice skating was Talia and Shawna's favorite sport.

All of a sudden, Talia didn't care about the cookies. She was upset because she didn't win the skating pass. "Oh," she said, "I wish I had won that." Talia was jealous.

It can be hard to be happy about someone else's good luck. ▶

Everybody Feels That Way

Everybody feels jealous sometimes. It can be hard to be happy for someone else's good luck when you want it too. But you can learn how to deal with feelings of jealousy and turn them around. You can start by focusing on good things that have happened to you. That way you can spend less time feeling angry and upset and more time feeling happy.

◀ Writing a list of good things that have happened to you may help you feel better.

Different Kinds of Jealousy

There are different kinds of jealousy. You might be jealous of a friend's good luck, like Talia was of Shawna's winning a free skating pass. You might feel jealous that someone else is getting the attention *you* want from a particular person. You might be jealous of something your friend or a classmate can do better than you.

You may feel jealous when a teacher pays attention to another student. ▶

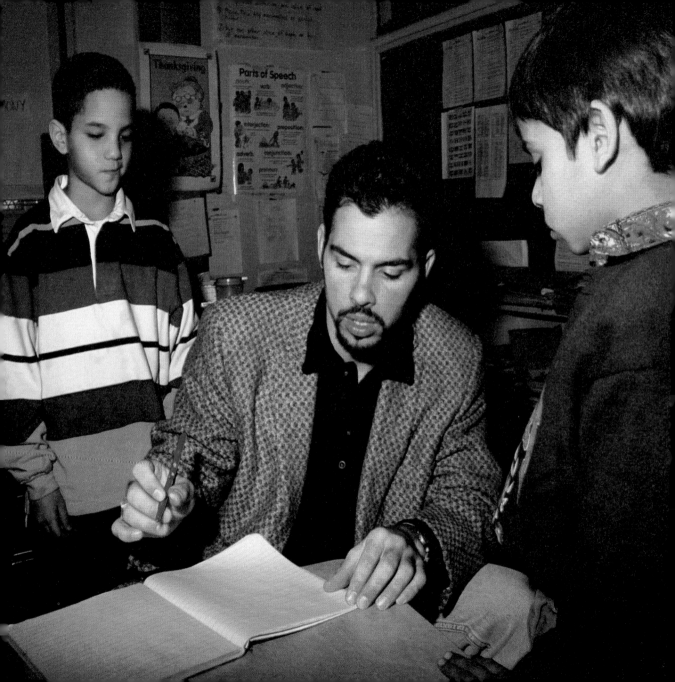

Paco and Jake

Paco and Jake signed up to play soccer. They never missed practice and couldn't wait for their first game. After the first quarter, Jake was pulled off the field. By halftime, Paco had scored three goals. Jake heard people talking about what a great soccer player Paco was. Jake felt jealous. He wished he could play as well as Paco. But then he remembered how much fun he had in practice. He decided that it was better to have fun than to worry about not being the best player.

◀ One way to stop feeling jealous is to focus on the good side of the situation.

Sibling Rivalry

You might find that you are jealous of your brother or sister. This is called **sibling rivalry** (SIB-ling RYV-ull-ree). It happens when you try to compete with your brother or sister.

Children in a family often want the same thing at the same time. It could be the last slice of pie or a chance to watch a favorite TV show. Kids often compete for their parents' attention.

Siblings often compete with each other. ▶

Eva's Story

Eva was home when her mom called and said Trent had broken his arm at recess. Eva ignored her brother when he came home from the hospital. She was feeling jealous about the fuss over him. "Doesn't anyone care about me?" she thought.

Eva shared her hurt feelings with her mom. Her mom hugged her tightly and said that she loved her very much. Eva began to feel better and went in to say hello to her brother.

◀ Telling your parent how you feel can help you feel better.

Expressing Your Feelings

Feeling jealous is normal. But it doesn't feel very good. You can learn to express your feelings in a healthy way. You can begin to get rid of jealous feelings by talking to someone about them. Your parents, teachers, and friends can help you. They care about how you feel. Choose a time when you can talk to one of them alone. Talk about how you feel. Ask for ideas on how to deal with your feelings.

If you are feeling jealous, ask your friend ▶
to help you deal with your feelings.

Feeling Good About Yourself

When you feel good about yourself and what you've done, it is easier to feel good about someone else. Someone who feels good about himself is **self-confident** (self-KON-fi-dent). You can increase your self-confidence by focusing on your own **accomplishments** (uh-KOM-plish-ments). If you feel good about what you've done, you can feel good about what someone else has done too.

◀ Feeling good about your accomplishments lets you feel good about others' accomplishments.

Proud to Be Me

Monica was excited. She had been chosen to perform karate for the visiting Japanese karate club. Her friend, Yolanda, was also chosen.

At the performance, everybody did their best. The visitors clapped and cheered for Monica. But Yolanda was given the highest award. Monica was proud of her own performance. She was also proud of Yolanda for winning the highest award.

Glossary

accomplishments (uh-KOM-plish-ments) Things you have done well.

emotion (ee-MOH-shun) A feeling.

jealousy (JEL-us-see) A feeling of resentment.

self-confident (self-KON-fi-dent) Feeling good about yourself.

sibling rivalry (SIB-ling RYV-ull-ree) Competition among brothers and sisters.

Index